W9-CKT-495

Science in Infographics
PLANTS

Jon Richards
and Ed Simkins

Gareth Stevens
PUBLISHING

Please visit our website, www.garethstevens.com.
For a free color catalog of all our high-quality books,
call toll free 1-800-542-2595 or fax 1-877-542-2596.

Cataloging-in-Publication Data

Names: Richards, Jon. | Simkins, Ed.
Title: Plants / Jon Richards and Ed Simkins.
Description: New York : Gareth Stevens Publishing, 2020. | Series: Science in
infographics | Includes glossary and index.
Identifiers: ISBN 9781538242797 (pbk.) | ISBN 9781538242810 (library bound) |
ISBN 9781538242803 (6 pack)
Subjects: LCSH: Plants--Juvenile literature. | Information visualization--Juvenile
literature.
Classification: LCC QK49.R47 2020 | DDC 581--dc23

Published in 2020 by
Gareth Stevens Publishing
111 East 14th Street, Suite 349
New York, NY 10003

Printed in the United States of America

CPSIA compliance information: Batch #CS19GS: For further information contact Gareth Stevens,
New York, New York at 1-800-542-2595.

CONTENTS

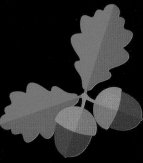

WHAT IS A PLANT?

Plants are living things that grow either on land or in water. They are usually fixed in one place and can use sunlight to produce the energy they need to grow.

TYPES OF PLANT

There are many different types of plant, but they can all be divided into two main groups:

Roses

Daisies

Deciduous trees

Flowering plants

These include most deciduous trees (see page 8), roses, and daisies, and make up most of the plant species. They produce fruit, seeds, and flowers, which are usually brightly colored to attract insects (see pages 22–23).

Fir tree

The seed-bearing, nonflowering plants include conifers, such as firs and pines.

Fern

Nonflowering plants

These can be divided into plants that produce seeds and those that reproduce using tiny spores.

Spore-bearing plants, such as ferns and mosses, spread their spores by releasing them into water or air.

Plants can also be divided by whether they are vascular or nonvascular.

Vascular plants

Vascular plants have thin tubes inside their stems, which transport water and nutrients around them. They include trees and ferns.

Nonvascular plants

Nonvascular plants don't have these thin tubes. They also don't have true leaves, stems, or roots. They include mosses.

The biggest individual tree in the world is a giant sequoia, nicknamed General Sherman. Found in California's Sequoia National Park, its trunk alone has a volume of 52,500 cubic feet (1,487 cubic m) – **that's about two-thirds the volume of a hot-air balloon.**

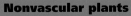

Watermeal

The world's smallest flowering plant is the tiny watermeal. Each one measures about 1 millimeter and could fit through the eye of a needle. A single thimble could hold about 5,000 of them.

Sewing needle

Scientists estimate that there are

390,900

types of plants known.

2015
2,034

21%

2,034 new plant species were identified in 2015.

21 percent of plant species are at risk of extinction.

PLANT CELLS

As with all living things, plants are made up of cells. A single plant will contain millions and millions of these cells and they dictate the plant's shape and how it behaves.

Chloroplasts – contain a chemical called chlorophyll that harnesses sunlight to produce sugars

Mitochondria – these use a process called respiration to produce energy using sugars and oxygen

Vacuole – a space inside a plant cell that contains sap and that supports the cell

Inside a cell

Plant and animal cells share many characteristics and structures, including a nucleus, a cell membrane, mitochondria, ribosomes, and cytoplasm. There are also several structures that are only found in plant cells, including a cell wall, chloroplasts, and a vacuole.

Nucleus – this is where the genetic instructions for the cell are stored, in a long strand-like chemical called deoxyribonucleic acid (DNA)

Cytoplasm – fills the inside of the cell and is where most of the chemical reactions take place

Ribosomes – tiny structures where proteins are processed

Cell wall – this is made from a tough substance called cellulose, which supports the cell

Cell membrane – this is the outer layer of the cell and controls what goes into and out of the cell

Scientists estimate that there are about **500,000 chloroplasts** in just **one square millimeter** of a leaf.

Stomata

On the underside of a plant's leaves are small holes called stomata, around which are guard cells. These cells can open and close to control the flow of gases and water into and out of the plant.

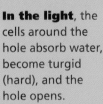

In the light, the cells around the hole absorb water, become turgid (hard), and the hole opens.

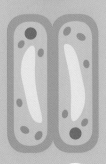

In the dark, the cells lose water, become flaccid (floppy), and the hole closes.

LEAVES

Most plants grow leaves, and they play a number of key roles in keeping the plant alive. Leaves are where most of the plant's energy production takes place, and also where the plant exchanges gases with the outside world.

DECIDUOUS LEAVES

Some trees, such as oak and plane trees, lose their leaves every year. They are called deciduous trees and they do this to save water during the colder months of autumn and winter.

Spring

Summer

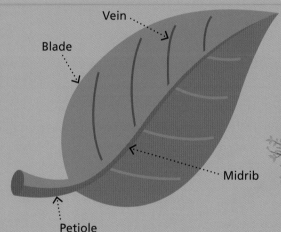

Vein

Blade

Midrib

Petiole

Autumn

Winter

EVERGREEN LEAVES

Some trees, such as pine and conifer trees, do not lose all of their leaves in autumn. Many of these trees are found in colder parts of the world where their conical shape allows snow to slide off easily so it doesn't cover the leaves for too long. The leaves are also very thin and narrow to reduce water loss.

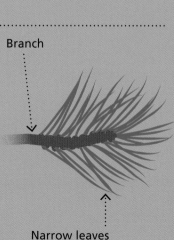

Branch

Narrow leaves

Inside a leaf

The leaf on a deciduous tree has a layered structure, with each layer performing different functions.

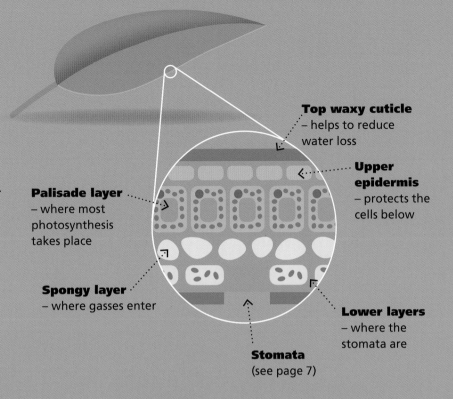

Top waxy cuticle – helps to reduce water loss

Upper epidermis – protects the cells below

Palisade layer – where most photosynthesis takes place

Spongy layer – where gasses enter

Stomata (see page 7)

Lower layers – where the stomata are

LARGE LEAVES

Leaves of *Raphia regalis* can reach more than 82 feet (25 m) long and 10 feet (3 m) wide. Each leaf is divided into about 180 separate leaflets.

The Amazonian palm *Manicaria saccifera* has some of the largest undivided leaves in the world, measuring 26 feet (8 m) across.

Math and leaves

The Fibonacci sequence is a number sequence where the next number is the sum of the two before it: **0, 1, 1, 2, 3, 5, 8, 13 …** Some plants grow their leaves and flowers according to this mathematical formula.

13
8
5
3
2
1
1

STEMS AND TRUNKS

Stems and trunks support the other parts of a plant, such as the branches and leaves. They are also the main highway along which the plant transports vital water and nutrients through thin pipes to every cell.

Vascular plants

Inside the stems and trunks of vascular plants there are thin tubes called the xylem and phloem. These tubes are used to transport water and nutrients to every one of the plant's cells, a bit like the blood vessels in your body.

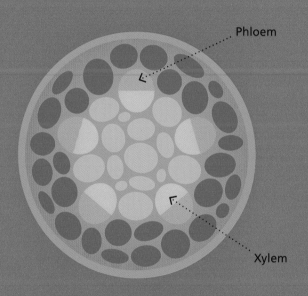

Phloem

Xylem

SUCKING UP LIQUID

Water moves through a plant using a process called capillary action. This is when the forces that hold the liquid together (cohesion and surface tension) and attract it to another surface (adhesion) are strong enough to overcome gravity. This draws the water up the thin tubes inside the plant's stem or trunk. In some trees, this action is strong enough to raise water more than 330 feet (100 m) aboveground.

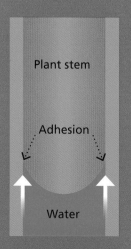

Plant stem

Adhesion

Water

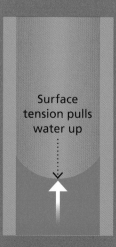

Surface tension pulls water up

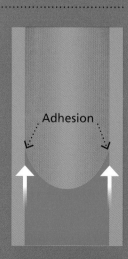

Adhesion

Growing rings

Many trees only grow during certain times of the year. Each year produces a growth ring inside the trunk – the older the tree, the more rings it has.

You can tell the age of a tree by counting its growth rings. Each ring equals one year.

Tree trunks have a tough outer woody layer called bark.

TALL TREES

A giant redwood nicknamed Hyperion is the tallest tree in the world. It is nearly 380 feet (116 m) tall, which is bigger than the Statue of Liberty.

380 feet

305 feet

Thick trunk

A Montezuma cypress in Mexico measures more than 98 feet (30 m) around its trunk. It would take about 18 people holding hands to form a chain around it.

UNDER THE SURFACE

Underneath the stems, branches, and leaves, and hidden from view, a plant's roots push down through the ground in search of water and nutrients. You might not be able to see them, but these structures play a vital role in keeping a plant alive.

Roots
A plant's roots play several key roles. These include:

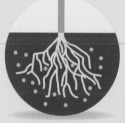

absorbing water and nutrients from the soil

anchoring the plant firmly in the ground

storing food reserves to use later

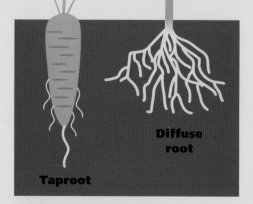

Diffuse root

Taproot

TAPROOTS AND DIFFUSE ROOTS
Some plants have a taproot, which burrows deep into the ground in search of water, while other plants have diffuse roots, which spread out in all directions.

Sucking in water
As plants move water up through their stems using capillary action (see page 10) and lose water through their leaves, they draw in more water into their roots from the soil.

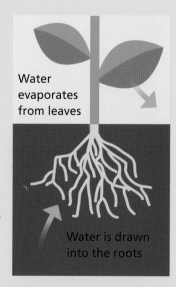

Water evaporates from leaves

Water is drawn into the roots

Root coverage

A colony of quaking aspen trees in Utah is formed out of a single organism that is joined together by one root system, making it the largest living thing on the planet.

Its root system covers 106 acres

– that's three times the area of the Pentagon Building in Washington, DC.

x3

It weighs 6,600 tons

– about the weight of 40 blue whales.

x40

Tubers

Some plants grow special underground structures called tubers. These are food stores the plant can use in times of shortage. These plants include yams, cassava, and potatoes.

Tubers

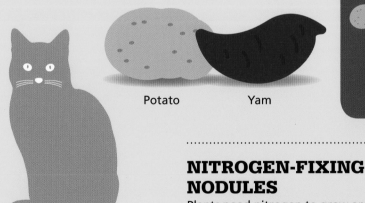

Potato   Yam

The world's heaviest potato weighed nearly 11 pounds

– about the same weight as a cat.

NITROGEN-FIXING NODULES

Plants need nitrogen to grow and some plants have the ability to take nitrogen from the atmosphere. They are called nitrogen-fixing plants and they use a bacterium called *Rhizobia*. The bacteria infect the plants, such as peas and beans, and store nitrogen in root swellings called nodules.

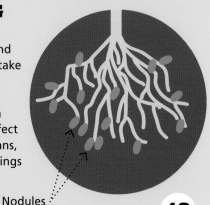

Nodules

PRODUCING ENERGY

Plants produce the energy they need to grow and survive in two stages. Firstly, a process called photosynthesis makes sugars. These sugars are then converted into energy in another process called respiration.

Photosynthesis

Plants draw water up through their roots and absorb carbon dioxide from the air. During photosynthesis, they use sunlight to convert these substances into a sugar (glucose), as well as oxygen, which is released back into the atmosphere.

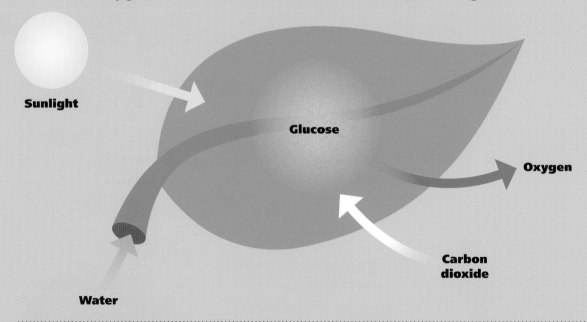

Sunlight

Glucose

Oxygen

Carbon dioxide

Water

CHLOROPHYLL

During photosynthesis, plants use a green chemical called chlorophyll to trap sunlight. This chemical is found in leaves and green stems. Even plants with leaves of other colors, such as red, purple, or yellow, photosynthesize. The chlorophyll is still present, but our eyes cannot see it.

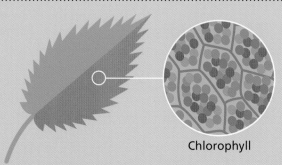

Chlorophyll

14

Scientists believe that tiny ocean plants, called phytoplankton, produce up to **85 percent** of the oxygen in Earth's atmosphere.

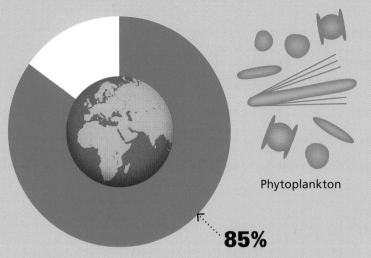

Phytoplankton

85%

Respiration

Plants produce energy during respiration, and this happens all the time, while photosynthesis can only happen in daylight. In respiration, the plant takes the glucose it made during photosynthesis and combines it with oxygen from the air. This process releases energy, as well as water and carbon dioxide.

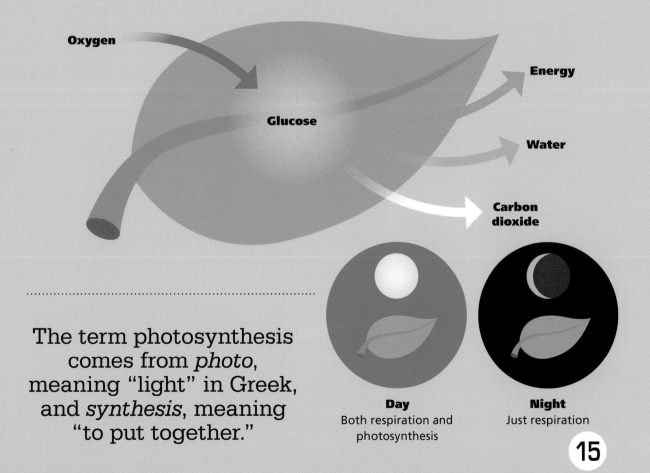

Oxygen

Energy

Glucose

Water

Carbon dioxide

Day
Both respiration and photosynthesis

Night
Just respiration

The term photosynthesis comes from *photo*, meaning "light" in Greek, and *synthesis*, meaning "to put together."

PLANT REPRODUCTION

Plants use many methods to reproduce. Some of these methods only involve a single plant, while others require at least two plants and even the help of small animals.

ON ITS OWN

Asexual reproduction only involves one parent plant. Some plants achieve this when their underground food storage organs grow into next year's plants. These plants include potatoes and daffodils.

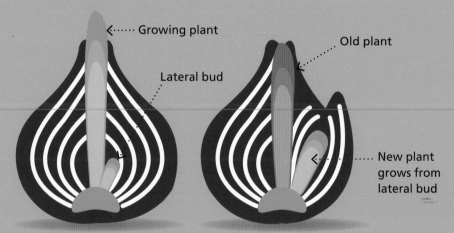

Growing plant

Lateral bud

Old plant

New plant grows from lateral bud

Other plants that reproduce asexually include duckweed, which produces small plantlets on its leaves, and strawberries, which send out runners from which small plantlets grow.

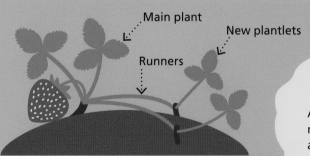

Main plant

New plantlets

Runners

Male and female

Sexual reproduction involves male and female plant cells merging. Flowers produce both male and female cells in different specialized parts.

Anthers produce male cells, which are called pollen

The ovary produces female cells

POLLINATION

Male cells, called pollen, are carried from one flower to another to merge with female cells in a process called pollination. Pollen can be carried on the wind or by animals, such as bees and other insects. The animals are attracted by a sugary nectar that the flower produces.

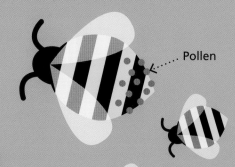

Pollen

Bees pollinate about
$15 BILLION
worth of crops in the US every single year.

Seeds

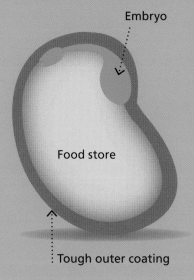

Embryo

Food store

Tough outer coating

The male and female cells merge in a process called fertilization. This merged cell develops into a seed. Inside the seed is the embryo, which is the young plant, and a food store, which the plant can use in the first few days of growth. Surrounding this is a tough outer coating to protect the seed.

The coco de mer palm produces the largest seeds in the world. Each one can measure 20 inches (50 cm) across and weigh 55 pounds (25 kg).

Dispersal

When the seed is ready to start growing, it has to leave the parent plant. There are several methods of spreading or dispersing seeds:

Self-propelled – pea pods spring open to throw out seeds

Outside animals – hooks on burdock seeds attach to animal fur

Inside animals – grape seeds are eaten in fruit and spread in dung

Wind – dandelion seeds are blown away by the wind

TREES

A tree is a large plant with a tall woody stem, called a trunk, which allows the tree to grow tall and not fall over. They are one of the most successful plants on the planet, and they cover huge regions, from the icy north to the lush rain forests near the equator.

TREES OR SHRUBS?

Shrubs have more branches appearing from close to the ground.

Trees have a longer stem or trunk, with the branches appearing some way from the ground.

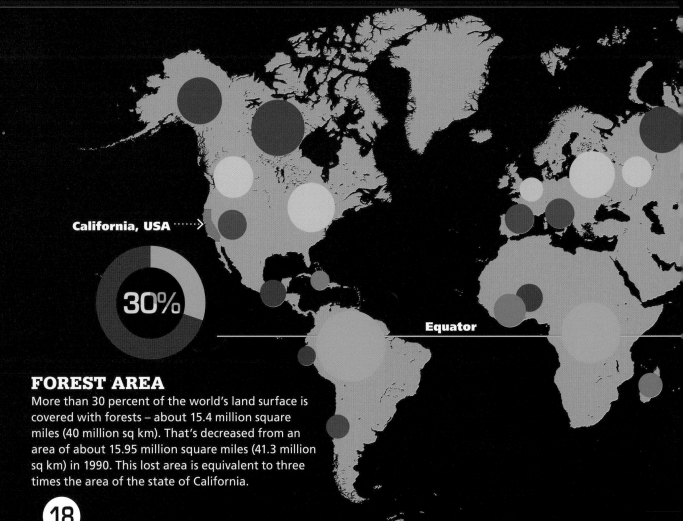

California, USA ······>

30%

Equator

FOREST AREA

More than 30 percent of the world's land surface is covered with forests – about 15.4 million square miles (40 million sq km). That's decreased from an area of about 15.95 million square miles (41.3 million sq km) in 1990. This lost area is equivalent to three times the area of the state of California.

Types of forest

Tropical rain forest – lush forest located near the equator

Subtropical forests – located north and south of tropical forests, they are found in areas with summer droughts

Mediterranean forests – most of the trees are evergreens and they are found in areas such as California, the Mediterranean, and Chile, with a short growing season

Temperate forests – a mix of deciduous and evergreen trees, they are found in regions with well-defined seasons, such as western Europe and parts of North America

Coniferous forests – found in cold regions close to the poles, they have a mix of evergreens and deciduous trees that can survive long, cold winters.

Montane forests – found in mountainous regions, they receive most of their water from mists and fogs that come up from lowlands

Plantation forests – managed forests that are grown for timber. They produce 40 percent of the world's industrial wood.

A large tree can lift up to 100 gallons of water out of the ground and into the air each day.

One tree can produce enough oxygen each day for up to four people.

That's enough to fill two and a half baths.

There are more than
23,000
different kinds of trees in the world.

GRASSES

At the heart of many of Earth's continents are large areas of grassland. These enormous seas of grass are found in places where too little rain falls for trees to sprout, or where huge herds of plant-eating animals prevent many trees from growing.

HOW DOES GRASS GROW?

While many plants grow from the tips of their stems or branches, grasses grow at each of the grass stem nodes and near the base of the leaves. This means that the tip of the grass can be cut, eaten, and trampled and the plant will continue to grow.

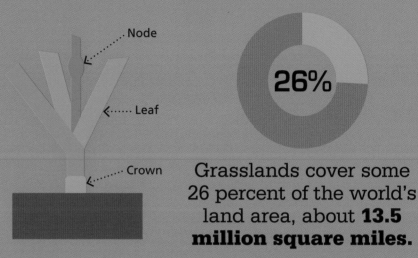

Node

Leaf

Crown

26%

Grasslands cover some 26 percent of the world's land area, about **13.5 million square miles.**

The rich soils of many grasslands make them ideal for farming and they are responsible for more than 70 percent of the world's agricultural area.

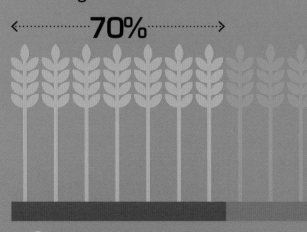

70%

Different names for grassland

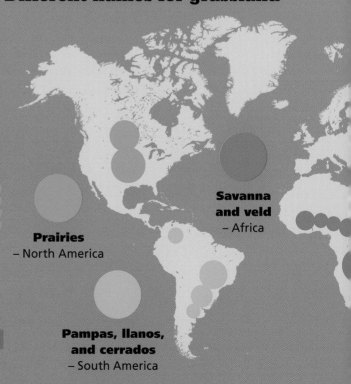

Prairies
– North America

Savanna and veld
– Africa

Pampas, llanos, and cerrados
– South America

Uses for grasses

As well as eating grasses, such as wheat, people find many other jobs for these useful plants.

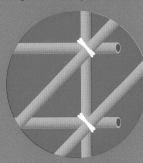

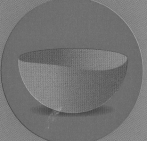

To make paper, such as papyrus in ancient Egypt

As scaffolding – bamboo is used in many countries in Asia

To make **thatching for roofs**

To make woven **containers**

Giant bamboo is the tallest grass plant in the world and some in India has grown to more than 150 feet (46 m) tall – that's almost as tall as the Arc de Triomphe in Paris, France.

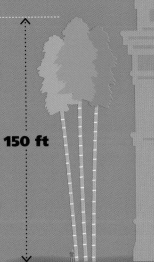
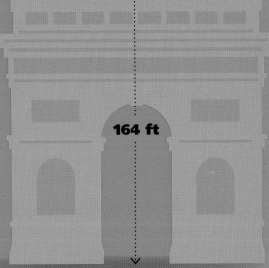

150 ft

164 ft

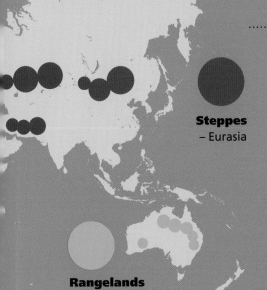

Steppes – Eurasia

Rangelands – Australia

There are more than

10,000

species of grasses growing around the world.

Species of **grasses** are found on every **continent**, including **Antarctica,** where **Antarctic hair grass** grows.

FLOWERS

Flowers play a key role in the reproductive cycle of many plants. Plants use a wide range of flower structures and strategies to make sure that pollen reaches their ovaries.

Giant flowers

Some plants produce enormous flowers to attract pollinating insects.

The titan arum produces a spike-like flower that can be 13 feet (4 m) tall and weigh 165 pounds (75 kg).

Rafflesia arnoldii produces flowers that measure about 3 feet (1 m) across and weigh about 15 pounds (7 kg).

Attracting pollinators

Flowers use several methods to attract birds and insects to pollinate them.

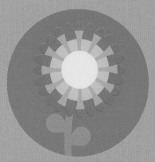

Birds and bees can see colors, which is why they are attracted to colorful flowers.

Many flowers produce a sweet liquid, called nectar, which birds and insects feed on.

Some flowers produce a pleasant scent to attract animals. *Rafflesia arnoldii* produces a smell similar to rotting meat to attract insects to help with pollination.

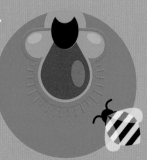

Some species of orchid grow flowers that look like female bees. Male bees are attracted to the flowers in search of a mate.

Some flowers, such as **sunflowers**, move during the day to **follow the sun** as it moves across the sky.

Some flowers have special patterns, called nectar guides, showing animals where the nectar is. These patterns can be seen in either visible light or using ultraviolet light, which some insects can detect.

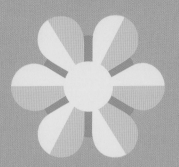

Flower in visible light   **Flower in ultraviolet light**

Of the **390,900** plant species known to science, **369,400** produce flowers.

94%

TULIP MANIA
In the Netherlands during the early 1600s, the bulbs of tulip flowers reached record prices, with some being sold for more than the price of a house at the time.

130 MILLION YEARS
– the number of years ago that the first flowers evolved.

PLANT PROTECTION

Plants contain lots of nutrients and water, making them attractive food for animals. Many plants have defenses to put off even the hungriest creatures.

Spines and spikes

Cacti have thick, juicy stems that are filled with water. These stems are covered with needle-sharp spines to put off thirsty animals.

Some cacti grow spines that are 6 inches (15 cm) long.

6 inches

Just **eight seeds** of the castor bean plant contain enough of the poison **ricin** to **kill an adult.**

STINGING HAIRS

Nettles have tiny hairs that can break the skin of an animal, injecting a mix of irritating chemicals that cause soreness and itching.

Hairs

Animal protection

Some acacia trees in Africa are home to several species of ants. The ants live inside the tree's hollow thorns and feed off the tree. In return, they swarm out in huge numbers and attack larger creatures that try to eat the tree.

Leaves fold up

Armor

Some plant seeds have a tough outer casing to protect them before they start to grow. For example, coconuts are covered in a thick, hairy shell to protect them as they fall from a tall tree.

CLOSING UP

Leaves of the sensitive plant *Mimosa pudica* fold up when they are touched. This stops grazing animals from eating the leaves and knocks off small insects that could damage the plant.

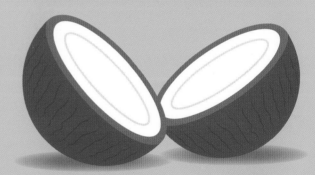

Poisons

Some plants produce poisonous leaves and other parts that can make animals sick and even kill them.

Hemlock

Aurum maculatum produces poisonous berries

Acorns are poisonous to horses

PLANT CYCLES

As with all living things, plants go through a cycle during their lifetimes. They develop from a seed, grow to maturity, and eventually die, but not before they reproduce to make more of themselves and start the cycle all over again.

LIFE CYCLE OF A FLOWERING PLANT

Germination – after a seed has left the parent plant, it waits until the conditions are right to start growing. This is called germination. The seed then grows small roots and a shoot

Growth – the roots and shoots continue to grow, producing more shoots and developing leaves

Flowers – the plant produces flowers that contain the sex cells

The plant fruits – after pollination, the male and female sex cells merge to produce a fertilized seed. Many plants produce fruit to protect and nourish the seed when it starts to grow

Seed dispersal – seeds may be spread by the wind or by animals

The plant dies – in some cases, the dead plant provides nutrients for its own seeds

Life expectancy
How long a plant lives can vary from one species to another.

Annuals –
complete their life cycle in one year

Biennials –
live for two years, growing in their first year, and then flowering and producing seeds in their second

Perennials –
live for several years

Monocarpic –
can take several years to reach maturity and will only produce one set of seeds

Some seeds wait a long time before germinating. One seed recovered from an archaeological site in Israel was found to be **2,000 years old.** It was planted and grew into a date palm.

4,800 YEARS

– the approximate age of the world's oldest tree, a bristlecone pine, nicknamed Methuselah. It grows in the White Mountains of California.

Fire
Some plants need fire as part of their life cycle.

Eucalyptus and banksias have cones and fruits that are sealed with resin. They need the heat from a fire to melt the resin and release their seeds.

After a fire, the remains of burned plants return nutrients to the ground. Some plants, such as the Australian grass tree, flower and grow quickly after a fire to take advantage of these added nutrients.

60 YEARS
– the length of time it takes a talipot palm to reach maturity before it produces flowers and then dies.

PLANTS AS FOOD

Plants are the most important source of food on the planet. While many herbivorous animals eat plants, humans eat grains, such as wheat and barley, as well as fruit, seeds, and pulses. We also grow crops to feed to farm animals.

Wheat
Wheat is a type of grass. Different types of wheat are harvested and used to make bread and pasta.

RICE
Like wheat, rice is a grass. When the plants are young, they are transplanted into flooded fields called paddies.

Rice is the staple food for half the people in the world and it is grown in more than 100 countries.

12,000 YEARS AGO
– when civilizations started to farm crops, choosing seeds from plants that grew best to increase the amount of food produced.

40,000
– the number of different types of rice

SUGAR

Sugars are found in many foods, including fruit (fructose) and milk (lactose). Two major sources of processed sugar are sugarcane and sugar beet. Sugarcane is grown in warmer countries, while sugar beet is grown in cooler ones.

Sugar cane

Sugar beet

HERBS AND SPICES

Some plants produce leaves, flowers, and seeds that can be used to flavor food. These herbs and spices include mint, rosemary, pepper, cinnamon, and mustard.

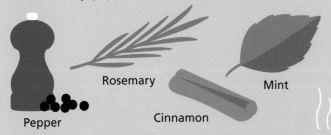

Pepper

Rosemary

Cinnamon

Mint

Coffee, cocoa, and chocolate

Cocoa and coffee beans are used to make drinks and sweets. Coffee beans are the seeds of the coffee plant. They are roasted to create the hard, dried bean that is then ground up and mixed with water to produce a cup of coffee.

Coffee beans

Cocoa beans

Cocoa beans are ground up to produce cocoa powder and also processed to produce chocolate.

Fruit and veggies

Fresh fruit and vegetables are an important source of nutrients, especially vitamins and minerals. Eating these nutrients helps to prevent many diseases.

Vitamin C – found in citrus fruit (such as oranges and lemons), broccoli, and potatoes. A deficiency can cause bleeding gums and a decreased ability to fight infections.

Vitamin A – found in carrots, tomatoes, and leafy greens. Prevents night blindness and skin rashes and helps your body fight off diseases.

29

GLOSSARY

adhesion
The force that holds particles from different substances together.

anther
The part of a flower where the pollen is stored.

capillary action
The movement of a liquid up a thin tube.

chlorophyll
The green substance in plants that enables them to use sunlight to produce sugars.

chloroplast
The small structure inside a cell that contains chlorophyll.

cohesion
The force that holds particles from the same substance together.

coniferous
Something that is made up of or related to conifer trees, such as a coniferous forest.

cuticle
The outer covering of something.

cytoplasm
The substance inside a cell that contains the tiny cell structures.

deciduous
A type of plant, such as a tree, shrub, or bush, that loses its leaves in autumn every year.

deficiency
When something is lacking.

evergreen
A type of plant that doesn't lose all its leaves in autumn.

extinction
When all the members of a species die out in a particular region or across the whole world.

germination
When a seed starts to grow into a plant.

growth ring
Also called an annual ring, this is a ring that forms inside a tree trunk during the growing season. One ring is added each year.

membrane
A flexible covering to something.

mitochondria
Tiny structures inside cells where energy is produced.

nectar
The sweet, sugary liquid that plants produce to attract insects and other animals to help with pollination.

nitrogen-fixing nodules
Small bumps on the roots of some plants. They contain special bacteria that process nitrogen, which the plant uses as a nutrient.

nonvascular plants
Plants, such as mosses, that do not have a network of tubes to carry water and nutrients.

nucleus
The structure inside a cell that contains the genetic information, or DNA.

organism
A living thing.

ovary
Part of a flower containing the female sex cells.

phloem
A tiny tube that carries nutrients around a plant.

photosynthesis
The process in which plants use sunlight, water, and carbon dioxide to produce sugars and oxygen.

phytoplankton
Tiny plants that live in the seas and oceans.

pollen
The male sex cells of a plant.

pollination
When a plant's male and female sex cells combine to eventually form a seed.

respiration
The process that uses oxygen and sugars to produce energy, water, and carbon dioxide.

spore
A tiny, single-celled unit that can develop into a new, adult organism.

stomata
Tiny openings that control the movement of gases and water into and out of the plant.

temperate
Refers to the parts of the world that lie between the tropics and the poles.

tropical
Regions on either side of the equator.

vacuole
A fluid-filled hole inside a plant cell.

vascular plants
Plants that have a network of tubes to carry water and nutrients.

xylem
A tiny tube that carries water around a plant.

Websites

MORE INFO:
www.dkfindout.com/us/animals-and-nature/plants/
This website has interesting information about many different kinds of plants.

easyscienceforkids.com/plants/
This web page is packed full of amazing facts about plants, from the structure of seeds to plants that eat meat.

MORE GRAPHICS:
elearninginfographics.com/category/k12-infographics/elementary-school-infographics/
This web page has tons of school-related infographics.

www.kidsdiscover.com/infographics
This website contains a whole host of infographic material on many different subjects.

Publisher's note to educators and parents: Our editors have carefully reviewed these websites to ensure that they are suitable for students. Many websites change frequently, however, and we cannot guarantee that a site's future contents will continue to meet our high standards of quality and educational value. Be advised that students should be closely supervised whenever they access the Internet.

INDEX